Less is More

Less is More

A Collection of Ten-Minute Plays

Edited by
David H. Rosen

RESOURCE *Publications* · Eugene, Oregon

LESS IS MORE
A Collection of Ten-Minute Plays

Copyright © 2016 Wipf and Stock Publishers. All rights reserved. Except for brief quotations in critical publications or reviews, no part of this book may be reproduced in any manner without prior written permission from the publisher. Write: Permissions, Wipf and Stock Publishers, 199 W. 8th Ave., Suite 3, Eugene, OR 97401.

Resource Publications
An Imprint of Wipf and Stock Publishers
199 W. 8th Ave., Suite 3
Eugene, OR 97401

www.wipfandstock.com

PAPERBACK ISBN: 978-1-4982-9759-2
HARDCOVER ISBN: 978-1-4982-9761-5
EBOOK ISBN: 978-1-4982-9760-8

Manufactured in the U.S.A.

CONTENTS

Acknowledgments | vii

Preface | ix
David H. Rosen

Contributors | xi

1 The Dissolution Mask | 1
   Nancy West

2 Thanatos Calling | 15
   David H. Rosen

3 Leap for Life | 26
   David H. Rosen

4 The Tea Gown | 32
   Maura Conlon

5 Baby Boomer Blues | 44
   Martin Cohen

6 Flip | 60
   Martin Cohen

7 True Blue | 71
   Eliza Roaring-Springs

8 Sisters | 83
   Eliza Roaring-Springs

ACKNOWLEDGMENTS

A debt of gratitude goes to Paul Calandrino, who taught an outstanding playwriting course at the Oregon Contemporary Theatre in Eugene, Oregon. Many of the playwrights in this book were in that class and benefitted greatly from Paul's input and inspiration.

PREFACE

In drama, as in life, it is important to get the point across quickly. Ten-minute plays do that. I have deep gratitude for these short yet essential plays. The reader will note that when you have ten minutes to get the essence across, it's quite powerful. One's philosophy can be summed up in just a few words. As I've grown older, I have an awareness that Shakespeare was right: "Brevity is the soul of wit." I think that you'll see what I mean when you read these plays aloud because spoken words ring true.

David H. Rosen
Eugene, Oregon

CONTRIBUTORS

Nancy West begin writing plays in 2012, and her plays have been produced at the world's largest short play festival, Short + Sweet Sydney in Australia, the Northwest Ten Festival of Ten-minute Plays at Oregon Contemporary Theatre in Eugene, Oregon, and Winter Shorts at Lane Community College in Eugene, Oregon. She has a degree in Theatre Arts from the University of Oregon, and has performed as an actor for more than 30 years. Nancy is a member of the Dramatists Guild of America.

David H. Rosen is the prolific author of fifteen books. He edited with Carol Goodman a recent volume titled *Darkness Holding Light: A Collection of Poems*. Other books by Dr. Rosen include *Transforming Depression: Healing the Soul Through Creativity* and the *Tao of Elvis*, both in their third editions. He also authored *The Healing Spirit of Haiku* with Joel Weishaus, which is in its second edition.

Maura Conlon is a writer, speaker and author of *The Los Angeles Times* bestseller, *FBI Girl*. People Magazines writes: "A refreshing antidote to memoirs about childhood trauma . . . A coming of age story that's at once universal and deeply individual." FBI Girl has been adapted for stage (Dramatic Publishing) with a forthcoming audiobook. Maura Conlon holds a PhD in Depth Psychology and lectures on legacy and the creative impact of life's first fourteen years. FBIgirl.com.

Martin Cohen, a playwright, director, and actor has been trained in theater at the Herbert Berghof Studio in New York City. He has also earned a Master's degree in Creative Writing at Oregon State University. As an actor and director, he worked with the Nomad's Theater, Los Angeles, and the Santa

Contributors

Monica Playhouse as part of their ensemble players. His roles ranged from Moliere to Ionesco to Albee.

His play, "So Far From Shore," about a 25 year old film director who was sexually molested as a child was produced for the stage in Springfield, Oregon at the Richard E. Wildish Theater. He has also written "Baby Boomer Blues," about the struggles and complications of learning to love ourselves, whose 10 Minute version was staged at the Oregon Community Theatre in Eugene, Oregon.

Martin's latest play, "Checkpoint," is based in part on Homer's Iliad, and involves the Middle East conflict between the Israeli and the Palestinian people.

Eliza Roaring Springs has been acting and directing and creating theatre for the last 40 years, but she has just recently discovered playwrighting. It's a whole new creative world to explore!

THE DISSOLUTION MASK
By Nancy West

Characters

LINDA 40s-50s, reserved, quiet, focused

BRIAN 20s-30s, on edge, emotional, wary

SETTING

A children's social service agency meeting room.

TIME

The present

Less is More

(LIGHTS UP on a rather worn children's social service agency meeting room. A few toys are visible. Posters are on the wall promoting immunizations in multiple languages. There is a short table for children. In the back of the room there is a large observation window with a one-way mirror, used for trainings, or to monitor visitations. In one plastic chair sits LINDA, carefully dressed, perched on the edge of the seat. She has kept her coat on. On the other plastic chair sits BRIAN. A beat-up backpack is by his feet.)

BRIAN

Where's George?

LINDA

He . . . he couldn't make it.

BRIAN

You didn't tell him did you?
    (LINDA is silent. BRIAN laughs. He digs into his backpack and pulls out a wrinkled piece of notebook paper, and nervously smoothes it out a little.)
OK, then, I wrote this down, so I wouldn't forget.

LINDA

I have to be back at work in an hour.

BRIAN

Sure. Sure. I don't want you to get in trouble. No, couldn't have that. OK. Question one.

LINDA

How many questions?

BRIAN

What?

The Dissolution Mask

LINDA

How many questions?

BRIAN

Well. Five. I have five questions.

LINDA

Five?

BRIAN

Five. What, if there were six, you wouldn't answer? That would be too many questions? Too personal, huh?

LINDA

No. I'm just . . . surprised that you asked to see me.

BRIAN

Why?

LINDA

Well, you were there. What can I tell you that you don't already know?

BRIAN

I don't remember everything clearly. I want to hear what you have to say. Question one. What did you do with all the money?

LINDA

Money? What money?

BRIAN

The thousands of dollars you got from the state for saying you'd adopt me.

Less is More

LINDA

Is that what this is about? Money?

BRIAN

I just want to know. They asked you to turn over any money in my savings account, and you sent them $30. Where did all that money go?

LINDA

To take care of you, to feed you, to clothe you.

BRIAN

You didn't save any of it? What if I wanted to go to college?

LINDA

Did you?

BRIAN

No. But that's not the point. You weren't poor. I moved in with you at nine, left at twelve. You could have saved some of it for me, for later. Why didn't you?

LINDA

Your foster mom Cheryl gave me some advice. She said kids who've been adopted need more physical space. So we bought a bigger house and paid a higher mortgage. We thought we had time to save later on.

BRIAN

Yeah, then it all "disrupted". Sounds real nice and clean. Like lancing a boil, eh? Easy.

LINDA

Dissolution.

The Dissolution Mask

BRIAN

What?

LINDA

It's called a dissolution, when it happens after the adoption is finalized.

BRIAN

Final. That's a laugh.

LINDA

I have questions, too.

BRIAN

Well, too bad. You agreed to answer my questions. I didn't agree to anything, you did. Question two. Do you have kids now?

LINDA

I'm not answering that.

BRIAN

Why not?

LINDA

Next question.

BRIAN

(Pause. BRIAN jumps up, crosses to glass window)
Why did you insist on meeting in this stupid building? I know you hate this place as much as I do.
(Pointing to window)
I know you hated how they watched you.

LINDA

There's better security here than at a coffee shop.

BRIAN

Because you think I'd do . . . what?
 (LINDA does not answer)
Question three. Did you love me?

LINDA

Yes.

BRIAN

Yes?

LINDA

Yes.
 (beat.)

BRIAN

You're lying.

LINDA

It's the truth. I—

BRIAN

How can you even sit there and look at me and say that? How can you—

LINDA

I'm not here to convince you—

BRIAN

You can't seriously expect me to just say, yeah, okay then—

The Dissolution Mask

LINDA

So why did you ask me if you already know the answer? Why did you fly halfway across the country to ask me a question you already know the answer to?

(Silence)

BRIAN

Question four.

LINDA

Brian—

BRIAN

QUESTION FOUR! Question four, oh, this is a good one. What is your happiest memory of me?

LINDA

One? One happy memory.

BRIAN

There must be one, right?

LINDA

Yes, of course. In fact, I brought something for you, a memento from a time that we enjoyed together.

BRIAN

What?

LINDA

You left it at the house.

Less is More

BRIAN

I thought you turned in everything that was mine.

LINDA

It was in a bottom drawer in our bedroom. I didn't find it until later, when we moved. It seemed too late to send it along by then. I didn't want to bother you or your new family. I thought you might want it. Do you?

(LINDA removes the shoebox from under her chair, and puts it on her lap.)

BRIAN

(Unsettled)
I don't know. You kept this? You had no right to keep anything.

LINDA

I thought—

BRIAN

Not one scrap. Nothing. I deserved to get it all back. It was mine. You had no right.

(Beat)

LINDA

We assumed you didn't want anything that reminded you of us.

(LINDA holds out the shoebox to BRIAN. He hesitates, then takes the box and opens it. He pulls out a painted paper-mache mask, the size of a child's face.)

BRIAN

A mask?

LINDA

Yes. Do you remember the day we made the masks?

The Dissolution Mask

(BRIAN shakes his head no)
First we put vasoline on your face, then the strips of quick drying plaster. I made one, and you made one. We helped each other. After they dried, we painted them.

BRIAN

Why did we . . . ?

LINDA

It was hard to find a project we could work on together. We didn't always . . . connect, and . . . it was sometimes awkward. I thought you might find making masks interesting. We were laughing, and telling jokes while we painted them. And then we put the masks on, and told stories.

BRIAN

Yes. Stories.

LINDA

Just silly stories. Fantasies. About boys escaping from castles and swimming moats. Running into the woods and finding a new tribe. Who rode unicorns.

BRIAN

Unicorns? That's . . . kinda creepy.
(BRIAN and LINDA laugh together.)

LINDA

We kept the masks on, and talked for a long time. I felt so close to you.

BRIAN

I don't remember the mask.

Less is More

LINDA

No. It only happened that once. You didn't want the mask in your room. You said it gave you nightmares. So it was in my room the night . . . the night you left.

BRIAN

What else is in here?

LINDA

A school photograph. And a note.

BRIAN

What note?

LINDA

You taped a note on my door saying you were sorry. I was angry because you stole my CD player. I never even acknowledged the note. I should have accepted your apology. I thought we had time.

BRIAN

You kept that note?

LINDA

Yes. I look at it sometimes. I keep it with the photo and the mask. It's all I have. But I brought them with me. I wanted you to have everything.

BRIAN

Why would I want that stupid note?

LINDA

Well, not the note, maybe, but I thought the mask—

The Dissolution Mask

BRIAN

I don't want anything from you! You gave me everything? You gave me nothing. You took everything. Question five. What happened?

LINDA

What do you mean, what happened?

BRIAN

What happened? Why did you get rid of me, really? Because of the fight?

LINDA

The details are in the police report, you can read that. Don't play innocent. You remember just fine. You always did.

BRIAN

Our old caseworker, Paul, I talked to him, he said it was just a fight, there was no reason I couldn't come home.

LINDA

Fight? There was no fight. George was at a conference. I was scared of you, of how angry you were, and while George was gone I locked the bedroom at night. I found the key to my bedroom in the pocket of your pants in the laundry. I confronted you and you attacked me, you kicked me down the stairs. My leg has never been the same. You kept coming after me, and I broke free and made it to the neighbors. You ran away. And we decided not to let you come back home.

BRIAN

You lawyered up, contacted the agency and got rid of me.

Less is More

LINDA

No! I made call after call to find you a therapeutic group home that could help you! But you had to be in foster care. I was scared of you, and I was scared we couldn't help you. We didn't think we had a choice.

BRIAN

What is this shit? These are all excuses.

LINDA

They are not excuses, they are explanations.

BRIAN

It's the same thing. It was easier because you didn't think I was really your kid.

LINDA

If it was another adult who hurt me, everyone would say, of course he couldn't come home. There would be no question. But because you were a child, you had no responsibility. Everything that happened was my fault.

BRIAN

It's still all about you, isn't it? I was the kid. You were supposed to protect me, and you kicked me out, and then you got a lawyer who said to stop calling you. You had my room all packed up and in the garage the week before this happened, so how can you even pretend you weren't looking for an excuse?

LINDA

Your therapist told us to do that. Every expert we talked to had their pet theory on how to help you. I have a question. Have you hurt anyone?

BRIAN

What do you—

The Dissolution Mask

LINDA

Have you hurt anyone else? Besides me?

BRIAN

What?! God, no, I would never . . . is that what you think about me?

LINDA

You were hurt. You were hurt in your first home. In foster care. You hurt me. Have you hurt anyone else?

BRIAN

No.
(LINDA is not convinced)
I have another question. Do you tell anyone about me? Or is it like I never existed for you?

LINDA

Question time is over. No more questions.

BRIAN

I want you to say you're sorry.

LINDA

I will say I failed you. That much is very clear. But no. I can't tell you "I'm sorry".
(BRIAN moves toward LINDA suddenly, in anger. She backs away. BRIAN turns and EXITS quickly, leaving his backpack on the floor and the shoebox on the table.

LINDA moves to the one way window, puts one hand over her eyes, and peers into the glass. She crosses to the table, opens the shoebox, removes the mask, and examines it. LINDA puts the mask up to her face and stands quietly, then removes the mask, puts it back in the box, and closes the lid.

The door opens suddenly, and BRIAN enters quickly. LINDA moves away, and turns her back to him. BRIAN grabs the backpack and starts to

Less is More

leave. He stops, looks at the shoebox, then looks at LINDA. BRIAN grabs the shoebox. BRIAN stops, considers. He opens the shoebox and carefully places the small piece of paper on the table.

BRIAN EXITS. LINDA turns back and looks at the note. She gently picks it up and holds it.)

(LIGHTS OUT. END OF PLAY.)

THANATOS CALLING
by David H. Rosen, M.D.

IN THE HONOR OF SAINT DYMPHNA

Cast

Doctor in his early 70s wearing a tweed jacket that needs to go to the cleaners and gold wire-rimmed glasses. He looks distinguished.

Claudia a widow in her 80s. She wears an all black sagging dress—it's clear that she has spilled something on the top half. Her shoes are bright red.

Setting

A small village.

Less is More

The doctor's office in his home is furnished *ala* the 1960s. It's clean and comfortable with two large chairs.

The audience hears a faint, eerie song of death. It's sort of like something you'd hear at a funeral, with a pastor saying, "This was her favorite song."

A doorbell sounds and the doctor opens the door and lets in a new patient. It's an elderly lady. He motions her to the closest chair.

DOCTOR

Nice to meet you Mrs. Moore, and I see that you got here without too much difficulty.

CLAUDIA

No problem, Doc, as you gave clear directions. It's fine to come here, as you take Medicare and that's all I have. My husband Thomas, but I always called him Tom, died two months ago. I've cried so much I feel like one of those springs that feeds a river. We'd been married for sixty years. He always said I'd outlive him and he was right. But not for long. I have a plan. Doc, I can see you're a nice man. Please call me Claudia.

She then plops down a loaded revolver on the little table between the chairs.

CLAUDIA

Why not? You tell me what's wrong with suicide. I wanna do it. I even have a permit for this gun. All of our dogs died. We had no children. My brother and sister are gone, so why live, Doc? I brought this gun, which I won't fire now, because I wanted to show you so you know I'm serious. It's loaded Doc. My friend Delores said, "Go see Dr. Snodgrass, he'll help you."

Doctor leans forward toward Claudia on the edge of his chair.

DOCTOR

Well, I'll do my best. That's very sad that your husband passed and you want to end your life.

Thanatos Calling

CLAUDIA

You got it Doc. Tell me why not. I've gone over this in my mind a hundred times. It seems clear to me. But I don't want to do anything violent. It's just not my way. Help me Doc.

DOCTOR

So why didn't you kill yourself? Why are you here? I can give you pills, but coming here and talking might help you.

CLAUDIA

Why do you say that? I'm near death so why don't I just speed it up? Give me some reason why not to shoot myself. Come on Doc. Look at me. What do you see? You see an old lady at the end of her life.

DOCTOR

I hear you, but, we are in this experiment called life, so why not complete it?

CLAUDIA

That's why I've loaded this gun. Tom showed me how before he died.

DOCTOR

I will help you figure it out.

CLAUDIA

Who's crazy? You're crazy! I'm eighty and I won't live much longer. If you don't like the gun, give me sleeping pills.

DOCTOR

But, why are you here?

CLAUDIA

I told you, to get pills. Or to shhhh. *She reaches for the gun but stops herself.* Let me kill myself right here. Then you can send me to the morgue.

Less is More

DOCTOR

Not so fast. *The doctor appears antsy.*
Please speak up. I'm a little hard of hearing.

CLAUDIA

Look Doc, I'm not gonna keep coming here. This is a one time visit. Just give me the pills if you don't want me using the gun.
Doctor thinks to himself
Why is she here? She could have ended her life with this gun. Or she could have just gotten aspirin over the counter.

DOCTOR

Are you having trouble sleeping?

CLAUDIA

Yes, and many more problems. Bigger. I piss and shit blood. You get it Doc?

DOCTOR

We'll get you admitted to our hospital and I'll have Dr.Zeitgeist help you. He's not a psychiatrist, but, is that what you want?

CLAUDIA

But why? I told you, I just want to go home and shoot myself with Tom's gun. Or I could do it here. He left it loaded in case of an intruder. Now the intruder is myself, and I'm going to end it all. Do you know the people at the funeral home?

DOCTOR

Medicine doesn't do that kind of stuff. We are here for life. Let's talk about your friend Delores, exercise and diet. Things that you have and things that you like. Do you paint or knit?

Thanatos Calling

CLAUDIA

I told you, I'm finished with life. I eat what I can afford that's on sale at the store. Thank God, Johnny's Market still delivers what I need. You know, cereal, milk, butter, and prepared meals that I heat up. But it's getting harder and harder with each passing day. And I told you, Doc, ever since Tom died, all I want do is join him. So tell me, why not?

DOCTOR

I hear you. But what keeps you going?

CLAUDIA

I don't know. I do like to feed the birds. Thank God I got rid of my cat. My dear Tom is gone and I miss him.

DOCTOR

What do you enjoy doing?

CLAUDIA

I told you, feeding the birds!
I'm sad Doc. But I can't fly, so why not die?

DOCTOR

Let's see if my friend Susan who's a social worker can help you.

CLAUDIA

How could anyone help me? I see what you mean Doc. I'm here and please give me the prescription. Are you just like those other helpers? They just push me down the hall.

DOCTOR

But, why not go to our nice hospital and get some tests to see what's wrong.

Less is More

CLAUDIA

I know what's wrong. I'm old and worn out. I mean you're no spring chicken, can't you understand?

DOCTOR

But the hospital is really set up for folks just like you.

CLAUDIA

What do you mean? Old people wanna die too. Don't you?

DOCTOR

There's a special wing for you.

CLAUDIA

What are you trying to say? That I'm . . . Is it a loony bin? I'm not going to a nuthouse.

DOC

Our hospital is not a nuthouse. *Pause.*
 Have you had any dreams?

CLAUDIA

What? What? Are you one of those dream doctors? Sure I have dreams. I die in my sleep. What does that mean, Doc? Seems pretty obvious to me. Didn't that Shakey guy say something about that?

DOCTOR

What are your dreams?

CLAUDIA

I told you, I die in my sleep. And it's not bad. I love it!

Thanatos Calling

DOCTOR

Are you religious . . . go to church?

CLAUDIA

I was raised Catholic. But it's stupid. It's supposed to be for families, but I can see that mostly it's old people sitting in the pews.

DOC

He hesitates. I really couldn't prescribe anything unless I understand your life.

CLAUDIA

But why live? That's the question. I have no kids. I'm sad. Hell, I cry all the time. You tell me, why not use what Tom gave me? I miss him. Was he saying, "Join me." Why'd he give this to me, Doc?

DOC

I don't think Tom would want you to kill yourself. *Pause.*
    Tell me what your days consist of.

CLAUDIA

I eat cereal after I get up. Then a piece of cheese like a little mouse for lunch. Dinner is easy, as I just put a thing we used to call a TV dinner in the oven. Now they call it something else. And they put on the outside, mostly organic. What does that mean? I thought everything was organic. I mean I'm organic, so are you Doc. What's the big deal? Why go on?

DOC

Let's find out what's wrong with you. I'll call the hospital. Can you get to the emergency room?

Less is More

CLAUDIA

No, unless you're gonna take me Doc. I just came here to get the pills. What's wrong with you? I told you. I don't wanna live anymore. Don't you have any other old patients, Doc? And what about your family? Is everybody okay?

DOC

My parents are deceased. I still have a sister and a brother. But we are not close. Like you I did not have children.

CLAUDIA

See! We are the same. We both suffer. You're gonna die too. Wake up, Doc!

DOC

Yes, I know. But we are here because of you.

CLAUDIA

Yeah, give me the prescription.

DOC

Now wait a minute. I'm not in the business of killing people. Rather, I save people who want to die.

CLAUDIA

Great, save me Doc.

DOC

Okay. *He picks up the phone and calls 911.*
911
What is it? How can we help you? Yes, I see on the phone that you're Dr. Snodgrass.

DOC

Yes, I am a geriatric psychiatrist.

Thanatos Calling

CLAUDIA

What are you doing Doc?

DOC

He puts his finger to his lips hoping to silence her.
　I have a patient right here named Mrs. Moore. She wants to die. She has a loaded gun and says she'll use it. Please come immediately to 877 Utopia St.

CLAUDIA

Yelling. I told you I just want a prescription. You're going too far by calling them. I'm going to use this on you. You're not doing what I want.
　They struggle for the gun, but Doc ends up with it. As 911 hears everything.

911

While we've been talking, I've notified all appropriate personnel to dispatch to your location.
　Sitting there in what was complete silence, they now hear multiple sirens approaching.

CLAUDIA

I knew I should have never come here. Damn you. All you wanna do is help. You're just like everybody else. I said I wanted to die. I came here to get the pills to do it. And then I was going to say my good riddance to the world. But no, you call the police.

DOC

I didn't call the police, Claudia. I called 911. Surely they'll send for an ambulance immediately. Then they will take you to the hospital.
　Claudia stands up and starts to go to the door.

CLAUDIA

Why did you do that? I'm leaving. You weirdo! All you doctors are the same.

Less is More

She tries to get the gun out of the doctor's hand, but he backs up quickly.

DOC

No! I'll hold it here.

CLAUDIA

No you won't, it's my gun. Tom gave it to me. Give it here!
With the gun he goes behind a chair.

DOC

No. I'll keep it and I'll give it back to you when you leave the hospital. I know you'll want to come back here to see me when you get out.

CLAUDIA

You liar.
She starts hitting the doctor with her purse.

CLAUDIA

Give me the gun! You son of a bitch! I came here for a prescription and you called 911. What kind of a doctor are you?

DOC

You know who I am and you must have known that you needed this kind of help.

CLAUDIA

Delores told me to come here. What kind of a friend is she?

DOC

I think Delores cares about you. Please sit down, let's talk more about it.

Thanatos Calling

CLAUDIA

What's there to talk about? I hate all of you doctors and social workers. I've met those kinds before. They come to your house. All I want is help with ending my life. I just want peace.
Doorbell sounds, then loud knocks on the door.

DOC

Someone's here. I'll let them in.
Claudia is taken away by police, ambulance, and social worker.
In a contemplative and reflective mood. In his chair alone. The doctor voices these thoughts.

DOC

Damn! This is an impossible profession. I wanted to help her, but not by aiding death. Yet, she has a point.

The End

LEAP FOR LIFE
by David H. Rosen, M.D.

Note to Readers

The following accounts are based on actual research. However, the names, dates, and ages have been changed to protect the privacy of the survivors and their families.

Character List
(in order of appearance)

Doctor	age twenty-eight, with a suede jacket and wire-rimmed glasses
Cathy	a single woman, age twenty, wearing a red dress
Hector	a single man, age nineteen, wearing a wrinkled long-sleeve dress shirt with faded jeans
Chuck	a widower, age twenty-six, wearing a dirty grey sweater
Sally	a terminally ill woman, age twenty-five, wearing a pink robe that needs washing

Setting

Backdrop: A huge photo of the Golden Gate Bridge.

Leap for Life

Beethoven's Moonlight Sonata is softly heard.
The action takes place on the Golden Gate Bridge between 1975 and 1982. There is a short railing between the walkway and the edge of the bridge.
The audience will see that the orchestra pit appears like water, but there is a net above the water.
The stage is empty. A bright light shines on a huge photo of the Golden Gate Bridge which covers the back of the stage. We see a railing also well-lit that you can easily step over.
A doctor stands mid-stage.

DOCTOR

The Golden Gate Bridge is a beautiful structure, and a modern wonder of the world. It opened in 1937 with a big celebration, but then the dark side began. Ever since, lost souls have been jumping to their death. The leap of about two hundred and thirty feet takes only four seconds. When a person hits the extremely cold water at 75 mph, no one is supposed to survive. As a young doctor at UCSF, I carried out a research project in which I interviewed ten of these survivors.

Dejected Cathy, just rejected by a lover, enters from stage left. She goes over the railing and stands on the ledge, contemplating before jumping. She voices her thoughts aloud.

CATHY

I should have never gone out with Clark. I did not know that he was married. And had two daughters, one of them was my age. There is no other way to deal with this pain and anguish. I was drawn to this place because it is a suicide shrine. It's majestic. The name pulled me here and I thought it was as good a way as any to enter heaven. He said we would get married, it would be a life of simplicity and grace. But it was a lie. That's why I'm here and that's why I'm no more. Working as a waitress was fun, but empty. Meeting the older man who seemed debonair was a bright spot in my dark day. When he asked me out, I hesitated. He came back several times, and the fourth time he asked me out, I said yes. It was like riding in a cable-car, but then the snap came. I fell out of love and I never saw him again. Becoming pregnant was a dead-end. I lost my identity. I thought about aborting the baby, then I decided to end both our lives. Suddenly it came to me:

Less is More

jump off the Golden Gate Bridge. What better way to save the baby from being born into a stressful life?

Cathy leaps to her death. Somber music accompanies her jump with cymbals.

Hector enters from stage left. He goes over the railing and stands on the ledge, contemplating before jumping. These are the thoughts that went through his mind . . .

HECTOR

I stand at the edge and know that this is the right thing to do. It's a horrible feeling . . . it's a terrible kind of despair to not know who you are. And that's why I decided to jump, because when you are nothing, nothing matters. I had bad parents. I was sexually abused by my mother and beaten by my father. It ended up making me crazy. I felt I was a lost soul. The only way out was death. That's what attracted me to this place, because I thought if I jumped off the Golden Gate, I would enter a spiritual realm. I was working for a contractor, but as I was building a physical house, my emotional house was falling apart. The medicine that the doctor gave me caused me to feel stronger. I liked the doctor and his medicine helped me feel better. Finally, I had the energy to kill myself.

Hector jumps to his death. His leap is accompanied by a loud pound on a bass drum.

Chuck enters from stage right. It's clear that he is grief-stricken, having just tragically lost his young wife to a hit and run accident as she was walking across a major street. He walks with his head down, shoulders bent, and looks like a deadman walking.

CHUCK

Betsy was the reason I was living. Without her, I entered a black hole. I was drawn to this eternal spot realizing that I could find light and be with her again by jumping. So I drove my car to the Golden Gate Bridge parking lot, and wrote a note explaining that this was an act of God. I felt like the light was connected with Him, and that would at least allow me to be with my loving wife again. Our baby girl allowed for the possibility of future grandchildren. I had the awareness standing there that this was a mistake, but the draw to be with Betsy was too strong. I went to see my pastor and received a passage from the Bible to read. "Whatever a man soweth, that shall he

Leap for Life

also reap." My depression was a malignant psychoma. Years of alcoholism, which started in high school, took its toll. Having a newborn gave me joy, but she could never replace Betsy. Thank God I could leave my daughter with my mother.

Chuck leaps to his death. You hear a loud crack of a snare drum.

Sally enters from stage right. She is gaunt, thin, and obviously terminally ill.

SALLY

Little did I know that hearing from my family doctor that I had cancer would end up this way. The visit to the oncologist was initially helpful. In the end, it was like a bandaid on a gaping wound. Looking back, the chemotherapy and radiation treatment seemed primitive. I liked Dr. Smithfield, but all physicians are limited in what they can do. Death is certain. It struck me that the abyss waits for all. Plants and birds became an extended family. My husband Jack was more upset than I was. It was crystal clear that nature was unquestionably accepting of my fate. Sharing my sadness with a giant oak was more comforting than talking with my doctors. The Golden Gate made sense. Reflecting on golden, it came to me that gold is eternal and everlasting.

Sally jumps to her salvation. The soft clash of cymbals is faintly heard.

Many years later each of the characters reported to the doctor their survival stories.

Sally enters stage right and stands facing the audience. Surviving spread joy all over her face.

SALLY

As soon as I jumped, I realized I made a mistake. I said to God, "I don't want to die, please save me." Living after leaping made me think immediately, 'why me?'. Am I special? Am I an angel? I have never felt extraordinary. This was the exception. Living after sure death caused an awakening that has persisted. I felt enlightened. It was way beyond anything I would have ever imagined. Going down deep in the darkness and feeling like I would freeze to death. I heard Elvis's "Why Me Oh Lord" echoing in my mind. Then, rising up with my head coming out of the water, being rescued . . . given a second chance, changed everything. Now wanting to end my life seems like pure folly. My cancer went away.

Less is More

Chuck enters stage right and stands facing the audience.

CHUCK

There is a God. Jesus appeared to me and looked just like He did in all the pictures. The next thing is a bit shocking to disclose, but it still feels good. It enables me to be here. Jesus embraced me, and I can still feel His presence. I have been advised to seek disability as I had some injuries. And I'm okay with it. Being disabled enables me. I'm cooking in a new way. Like my Lord, I want to serve, and I've developed a route where I give to the homeless. It's so gratifying to give bread that I made to those lost souls. My days end at the mission, where I help prepare the evening meal and talk with my dear friends. It is pure grace that Betsy will be able to enjoy all this with me. It is a blessing that I will watch our little girl grow and develop into a young woman.

Hector enters stage left and talks to the audience as if it were family.

HECTOR

At first, everything was black, then grey-brown, then light. It opened my mind --like waking up. When the sea lion nudged me up to the surface, I realized I was alive. I felt reborn. I was treading water and singing -- I was happy. Surviving affirmed my belief that there is a higher spiritual world. I felt chosen because I didn't die. I was thankful. I cried in the hospital and with my family. I cried a lot. I decided to serve others. I realize now how powerful God is and how little we are, and that it's not up to us. I felt somehow I was aiding others in the spiritual realm.

Cathy enters stage left and stands facing the audience.

CATHY

I'm torn asunder because my baby died. But I'm grappling with the fact that I'm still alive and I can have a new baby. Before I jumped, I was an agnostic—no real belief in God. After the leap, I became fully religious. I believed in God; He accepted my baby. He became a living reality for me. It's beyond most people's comprehension. I now know the meaning of life—like watching a bird fly—everything is real when you come close to losing it. I experienced a feeling of unity with all things and a oneness with all people. After my rebirth, I feel for everyone's pain. Surviving confirmed my belief and purpose in my life. Everything was clear and bright—I became aware of my relationship with my Creator.

DOCTOR

By surviving, Cathy, Hector, Chuck, and Sally wound up committing symbolic suicide instead of actual suicide. In retrospect, they each realized that they had planned their jump in a confused and demoralized state, during which they had defined their whole being in terms of a specific wound, failing, or negative self image. All ten survivors that I interviewed recommended that a barrier be constructed on the Golden Gate Bridge. In every case, I interpreted this plea as a projection of an inner barrier against suicide. None of these people went on to kill themselves. People can overcome suicidal depression. In this way, these near-death individuals were transformed. Thank God for the 'Eureka' experience of the Golden Gate Bridge Authority and their decision to put up a net in order to catch any lost soul who jumps.

THE TEA GOWN
by Maura Conlon

Characters

NAOMI Early 30s. Living in Brooklyn with husband, Mike, she's working now as a caterer.

MIKE Early 30s. Left old career to start an import/export business and married to Naomi for six years.

EVA Turkish seamstress, 60s, beautiful, schooled in the old country.

Setting

A gray New York late afternoon inside a yellow apartment

Time

Modern day

The Tea Gown

Mike enters the apartment holding a beret, suitcase, a binder with fabric samples and measuring tapes. Seeing Naomi, he throws everything on the sofa, opens his arms. Naomi is broiling.

NAOMI

I was looking at our account this morning—ten thousand dollars has gone flying out. Perhaps there's something you'd like to tell me?

MIKE

Oh. Yes. That! Fabric dealers in Istanbul requested a last round of investment and all partners on board. Finally, we have an exclusive with—

NAOMI

*Ex*clusive? What about *includ*ing your wife in decisions that jeopardize our future. I can't believe you just went, la-di-da, and did this—

MIKE

I'm trying to maintain important connections—

NAOMI

Oh, I see.

MIKE

We've jumped the last hurdle. Now that the papers are all signed, the distributors nailed, and all that other—well, voila! Soon, I can start filling orders.

NAOMI

You were supposed to come home *with* orders. Instead you've wiped out our savings.

Less is More

MIKE

These guys, they're the masters, a dying breed. And their enthusiasm to do business with me, the great-grandson of Theodore Pamuk, from Istanbul himself, well, honey—that's just way off the charts.

NAOMI

You and your dead ancestors! Mike, did anybody ever tell you, that you are so, *soooo*—lost.

MIKE

I was going to text you. We were just finishing up, then I headed to the airport, to come home, to see you. You've been so patient.
(He reaches for her, she resists.)
We're in this together. Another few short years/we'll be rolling in the moola—

NAOMI

You could have been working as a doctor right now.

MIKE

But darling, now we're in textiles.

NAOMI

You are in imports/exports.
(She steps away from him.)
You could have been a physician. That was your last big dream.

MIKE

How much longer do I need to apologize? Okay. Sorry. Hold it against me for the rest of my life: It took four years of medical school and a year of residency to realize I hated taking care of whining patients.

The Tea Gown

NAOMI

Patience? Yes. I'll tell you about patience. I stopped everything—left culinary school, moved across the country—twice. So, what about *my* needs? What about *me*?

MIKE

You?

NAOMI

Yeah, that's spelled: *m-e*. The opposite of You, which is spelled *one crazy ass*. My big catering affair is in two weeks. Big media will be there, even British royalty.
(She walks to table, picks up portfolio.)
You know I have had my sights set on wearing that tea gown.

MIKE

That tea gown?

NAOMI

Yes, Mr. Textile Man.
(She lifts up the illustration, flashes it to him.)
Remember how I showed you, the night we were putting together the numbers, talking about our budget?

MIKE

Oh, that night. Why is it we always talk about budgets at night?

NAOMI

I swear . . . I was taught to never covet anything in my life—but I *covet* this dress. It alludes to a woman's form so well—the mystery. Oh, this is how I want my clients to remember me! Mystery builds business.
(She twirls once as if modeling the gown.)

Less is More

NAOMI (cont'd)

Imagine me: chatting with the Queen while wearing Designer, Jessie Franklin Turner, Vintage Tea Gown. Silk. 1926. The real deal . . .

MIKE

Sorry, honey. Maybe some other dress will do.

NAOMI

Well, I'll admit: I'm not surprised. Not at all. The world revolves around your little/cockamamie/ancestral business. 24/7/365. Anyhow—I've met someone, with connections.

MIKE

You've met someone? . . . With connections?

NAOMI

I'm going to need them. Why couldn't have we used some of the money for my dream job? Life would have been easier if you'd stayed a doctor. We could have been . . . settled.

MIKE

But darling, people change.

NAOMI

Yes, so they do—*Another* five years? Is that when you become your highfalutin import/export king? You have anything to say for yourself, Mike Pamuk? Think quick. Quick is all you got.

MIKE

Well, I/you/we . . . things . . . are in transition—

The Tea Gown

NAOMI

That's a lovely word. Transition! It must be a gas, flying off to Istanbul, smoking hookah, speaking French like some ex-pat. And I stay put. Chase down leads. Now I have an *actual* big contract and, well/not that they speak god-damned French in Turkey, but *you* do! Get on the airplane with your beret, Mr. *Bonhomie*.

MIKE

Are you having an affair?

NAOMI

An *affair*. I am planning for an affair, Michael. I'd really like to plan for one. I need that tea gown. I asked you so very plainly. Perhaps a birthday gift? Yes, a few thousand dollars. But it will last a lifetime. Can you oblige me? No. What was I thinking?
(She juggles with his textile samples, allows them to drop all over the floor. He gasps, falls onto hands and knees, picking them up.)

MIKE

Careful! For god's sake—These are great Grandpa Pamuk's originals. Rich in history. Delicate. *Craft.*
(He stands, putting textile samples in neat pile. He reaches out toward her with one sample.)
The world is *losing* craft. I can bring it back! Ah, feel that texture, fine-spun, soft as a breeze. Soft, like your cheeks, Naomi. God, isn't that a gorgeous smell—

NAOMI

Sure, if you prefer hashish.
(The phone rings and catches both of them by surprise. MIKE remains frozen in place. NAOMI picks up, speaking into phone.)

NAOMI (cont'd)

. . . Yes, yes. I'm glad you called. Sure I can meet you in an hour. Columbus Circle? I know the café. Fantastic. *(Whispers)* Can't wait. *(Hangs up)*

Less is More

MIKE

Would you mind telling me what's going on?

NAOMI

I need to go. Pizza's in the oven.

MIKE

I'm home not even one hour after being gone ten days, tired as all piss. And now you're taking off.
(She walks over to oven, pulls out the pizza and places it next to an empty plate on the table.)

NAOMI

Pizza's out of the oven. I'll be back in a few hours. You're jet lagged. Get some rest.
(He stops her as she attempts to walk past him.)

MIKE

What do you take me for, a *fool*?

NAOMI

A fool? Ah, that infamous, four-lettered, *F*-word.

MIKE

Come on, let's sit down, talk for crissakes. You didn't tell me you were so unhappy.

NAOMI

My affair is in two weeks. I've got a lot to do . . .

MIKE

Your *affair?!* I thought it could always be, me and you, you and me—you know—having the affair.

The Tea Gown

NAOMI

Oh, please. My debut attire: The tea gown. I've met someone, with . . .

MIKE

Yes, connections—

NAOMI

—in the industry. You should like that . . . maintaining an important connection. *Ha!* Even I can do a French accent, if I must.
    (*NAOMI walks to mirror, applies red lipstick, searches for purse. Just then, the apartment buzzer rings.*)

MIKE

I'll take care of this.

NAOMI

Take care of what?

MIKE

My last bag never arrived. Probably the airlines delivering it. (*He checks his watch.*) Six o'clock. Right on schedule. *Oh*, I'll leave the door unlocked, for when you return. If you return.

NAOMI

(*Flummoxed*)
I'll see you later.
    (*Beat. The moment when the couple used to kiss when one of them left the apartment. Now they stare at one another. Naomi grabs her purse, brushes past him. Then, a knock on door just as she touches the knob.*)

NAOMI

You'll handle this?

Less is More

(NAOMI opens the door where a woman in her late 60s stands, jeweled, stately, tailored, her hair in an elegant braid.)

EVA

(In a thick European accent.)
Hello. This is the Pamuk apartment, yes?

NAOMI

You're with the *airlines*? Wow, I didn't know they had people like you... *Uh*, that's my husb—, Mr. Pamuk, the one with the *lost* luggage.
(EVA bows, holding an old-fashioned suitcase.)

EVA

And you must be Miss Naomi?

NAOMI

If you'll excuse me—I'm out of here.
(Looks at MIKE who crosses his arms and sits in a chair.)
Can you at least take care of *this—*

EVA

(As if reading a crystal ball)
I hear, Miss Naomi, that you are having an Affair.

NAOMI

I've got to be in the city in 30 minutes. Madam Luggage Deliverer—thank you—good night.

EVA

Miss Naomi, this suitcase is for you—it has your name on it. "Naomi Mac-Govern Pamuk." It is, special delivery.

The Tea Gown

MIKE

Hmmm.

NAOMI

I'm sorry, but there must be some mistake. Mike, please—aren't you going to handle this—*please?!*

MIKE

But darling, it appears you've got a gift waiting. You wouldn't want to leave just yet—not before you open it—would you?

NAOMI

I am expecting nothing.

EVA

Madam Naomi, I shall be more precise. What's in the luggage is for your Affair.

NAOMI

My affair? My affair! How do you know about my affair?

EVA

Your husband told me.

NAOMI

But he's been in Turkey.

EVA

As have I.

NAOMI

Who are you? I'm going crazy. No I'm not. I am leaving. Good-bye.

Less is More

EVA

Your big Affair in two weeks, madam.

MIKE

Please take the luggage, Naomi.
(NAOMI paces, then tosses her purse on the couch. She takes the suitcase from EVA, hesitates.)

MIKE

Time's a' wastin'. You going to open it, or not?
(NAOMI sits on couch, unlocks the suitcase and opens it. She wades through piles of tissue paper. She gasps when she uncovers what's underneath, buries her face into folds of sparkling silk fabric. She can barely lift her head.)

NAOMI

Oh. My. God. It can't be—

EVA

Your husband came to my couture shop, in Istanbul. He showed me the picture of The Tea Gown. I arrived JFK today, business here . . . *(beat)* Imports/exports. *(beat)* And now, if you will excuse me, I have a niece waiting downstairs.
(EVA bows and exits. MIKE stands, closes the door. Pauses. Then opens the door and steps away.)

MIKE

No doubt you will have an Affair to remember . . . Or, Naomi, *are* you?
(She stands up, holding the tea dress high in the air, feeling its fabric, jewels, gold casing, draping against her body, nearly speechless.)

NAOMI

This is/I—You . . . are/Oh My!

The Tea Gown

MIKE

You'll be dressed as a queen yourself.

NAOMI

Oh, Mike. You are maintaining an important connection.
(She slips on the tea gown over her black shirt and leotards.)

NAOMI (cont'd)

It fits exactly as my body had dreamed.
(NAOMI, exuberant, waltzes her way toward MIKE, who stands by the opened apartment door. She kicks the apartment door closed with her heel.) She twirls.)

NAOMI (cont'd)

Mr. Pamuk, you are my affair to remember.

MIKE

(A long exhale.)
Vintage silk. Designer Jessie Franklin Turner, 1926.

NAOMI

The tea gown.

MIKE

The real deal.

NAOMI

(to Mike)
Yes, the *real* deal.

The End

BABY BOOMER BLUES
by Martin Cohen

Characters

DAN A struggling playwright, dreamer all his life. At age sixty, and having two adopted children, he is experiencing a mid-life crisis wanting to father a biological child. DAN is somewhat comfortable being a child himself.

GRANDPA DAN's father, middle eighties, lives with DAN. Was a hoofer and still retains theatrical deportment and style. He speaks with a broken East European accent.

CHRIS DANs adopted daughter, age 13, outgoing, warm and very vulnerable.

Time

Present.

Setting

Living room of a large city apartment.

Baby Boomer Blues

The scene opens in DAN's apartment. GRANDPA dressed in colorful Bermuda shorts and a winter jacket buttoned up to his neck, is seated in an easy-chair with the newspaper spread across his lap. He is dozing with his mouth wide open. The radio is a blaring hard rock song. DAN enters the front door. He places his coat in the hall closet and switches off the radio. GRANDPA jumps awake.

GRANDPA
Hey, what you do? I listening to my music.

DAN
You were sleeping, Dad.

GRANDPA
You betsha. I sleeping and I listening!

DAN
How can you be sleeping and listening at the same time?

GRANDPA
How you can be college graduate and big dummy at same time?
(DAN smiles and starts toward the radio)
NO! I got headache from that damn music!

DAN
Sure, Pop.

GRANDPA
What I doing here? My house in Florida. I'm cold here.

DAN
Don't you remember why I brought you here?

Less is More

GRANDPA

I remember good! Aaach! I no remember . . . NOTHING!

DAN

Sure you do, Dad. You remember knocking on aunt Dina's door at twelve midnight.

GRANDPA

I go her house every night for dinner.

DAN

Yeah, at 6 o'clock, not twelve midnight!

GRANDPA

Sometimes I loose track time. *(Upset)* You think I got Alzheim?

DAN

They say if you remember enough to ask, you don't have Alzheimers.

GRANDPA

You betcha! I no have . . . too young! So why I can't remember nothing? Can't remember where I put . . . wallet . . . medicine . . . teeth.

DAN

Didn't I buy you a basket to put your things in?

GRANDPA

Don't remember where I put basket!

DAN

(The telephone rings. Dan picks up phone.)

Bueno?... Que pasa?... thanks sweetheart. My Spanish is coming along, isn't it! *(To GRANDPA)* Christine.... I'm O.K. How, eh... Oh sweetheart, what's the matter? Are you crying?... Sure we can talk about it... I want you to come here... Yeah, now. I'm not going anywhere. I'll be right here waiting for you... Christine?... Can't you come over now?... You get me all upset hearing you cry like that and then you tell me you're busy. Can't you go shopping some other time?... I know it makes you feel better, but that's not going to help what's bothering you... Do you want me to come over there?... Then you better come here, and pronto. I'll be waiting with a big hug and a kiss. Adios... I love you too.... and yes, I have something to tell you.
(He hangs up phone)
She's still upset about something we talked about.

GRANDPA

So you told her about...

DAN

No. I didn't tell her. I didn't have it straight in my head. I started to talk about it, but all I could say was that there will soon be some changes coming up for our family. She didn't go for it and got upset at me for "creating unnecessary drama" in her life!

GRANDPA

So now you have straight head on you shoulders!

DAN

I think so. I've done a lot of thinking...

Front door flies opened and Chris rushes in throws her coat and bag on the coach and exchanges heart-felt hugs with DAN.

CHRIS

Hey!

DAN

That was quick.

CHRIS

I was just down stairs when I called. Grandpa, how are you?

GRANDPA

Fine. You?

CHRIS

Fantastic! So how do you like living here with Dad?

GRANDPA

You father stink-up bathroom . . .

DAN

Dad!

GRANDPA

. . . otherwise . . . he perfect roommate!

CHRIS

I bet you miss Florida.

GRANDPA

Soon I go back.

DAN

No, Dad, you're not going back.

Baby Boomer Blues

GRANDPA

Soon I go back to be with you grandmother.

CHRIS

No Grandpa, you're going to live a long time.

GRANDPA

I old man.

CHRIS

No you're not, Grandpa. You're a youngee. Dad tells me you listen to rock and roll music.

GRANDPA

Helps put me to sleep.

CHRIS

Promise you won't go back for a long time, Grandpa. I would miss you so much.

GRANDPA

You grandmother was big nag when she alive and bigger nag calling to me from grave. She wait this long, she can wait till I ready.

CHRIS

That's the spirit Grandpa. *(Pause)* I need to talk to Dad. Can I ask you to go to your room so I . . .

GRANDPA

"Go to your room." Now I know I in second childhood.

Less is More

DAN

Chris!

CHRIS

I just want us to have a little privacy, Dad.

GRANDPA

You betsha. Call me when my "time out" finished.
Exits

CHRIS

I love you, Grandpa.
(To DAN)
He's so cute.

DAN

(Sour expression)
Yeah, cute!

CHRIS

(Imitates GRANDPA)
You betsha. So what you want talk me about?

DAN

Not bad! "You should be on the stage. It's a shame
(They finish together)
the last one left for Tucson an hour ago."

CHRIS

Jeez, Daddy, you are so lame.

DAN

Never mind. Is it true you stopped flushing the toilet?

Baby Boomer Blues

CHRIS

WHAT? Where did that come from?

DAN

Simmer down lassie. Your mother asked me to talk to you. Seemed pretty upset. She said you're driving her crazy . . . refusing to flush the toilet.

CHRIS

Oh, God ! . . . I flush the toilet . . . only not every time.
(With true conviction and in one breath)
Aren't you aware, dear father, that there's a water shortage and one shouldn't flush the toilet every time you take a pee because water is our most important renewable resource, and . . .

DAN:

OKAAAY!

CHRIS

Why, you think you're so innocent? You and Mom used to get into it over the . . . toilet seat.
(Imitating Mom)
"For God's sake, Daniel, why can't you remember to put down the damn toilet seat after you go."

DAN

Got me! But please stop intentionally pissing off your mother.

CHRIS

(Flaring up)
I wish you would say, "Mom" instead of "your mother," as if she were a stranger . . . And I am not "pissing-off," as you so crudely put it, "my mother," . . . at least not intentionally.

Less is More

DAN

You guys have enough trouble getting along as it is.

CHRIS

Oh! I hate when you criticize Mom.

DAN

I am not criticizing Mom. I'm merely . . . I'm . . .

CHRIS

(Abrupt change. Completely sincere.)
You think you and Mom will ever get back together?

DAN

You have to be tired of asking.

CHRIS

No, not really.

DAN

Okay . . . The reason I asked you . . . (Long pause)

CHRIS

Yes, Daddy, I'm listening.

DAN

. . . the reason I asked you to come over . . . ah . . .

CHRIS

Is this going to be bad, Daddy?

Baby Boomer Blues

DAN

No, not at all . . . well, I'm counting on you to take this in the right way.

CHRIS

It's going to be bad, isn't it?

DAN

I met someone . . . a young woman . . . and we have become, well, very close. . . . And I'm going to ask her to marry me.

CHRIS

I don't understand. Why do you want to marry a young girl.

DAN

She not a girl, she's a woman . . . and I want to marry someone young enough to have my baby.

CHRIS

WHAT? You want to have a baby with this person?

DAN

Yes, I do, Chris.

CHRIS

How old is . . . this young woman? Is she older than me?

DAN:

(Trying to be patient)
    Yes, she's thirty-three.

CHRIS

But you're twice as old as her.

Less is More

DAN

Not quite . . .

CHRIS

I don't understand . . . a child? Why are you doing this? You have me and Matthew. We're your children!

DAN

Please give me a chance to explain. . . . You know I love you and Matthew. You're my children . . .

CHRIS

But not like a biological child . . . is that what you're saying?

DAN

No! That's not what I'm saying!

CHRIS

(Screams) THEN WHAT ARE YOU SAYING? First you divorce Mom and ruin the whole family, then you want a child, at age sixty, when you already have two children. Why don't you just say we're not good enough?

DAN

No, I'm not saying . . .

CHRIS

Adopted children are not good enough. You tricked us. You're not my real father. *(Moves to pick up her coat and bag.)*
    Oooooh!
(Exits out front door. After a beat, CHRIS re-enters)
I HATE YOU!
(Exists and slams door behind her)

Baby Boomer Blues

DAN

(Looks up)
Hello . . . God, are you there? I know how busy you are, and I don't want much of your time, but I have this crises down here . . . and I need some guidance . . . God?

GRANDPA

(Voice of GRANDPA off stage in deep, God-like, tone)
I never give problem you no able to solve.
(Enters)

DAN

Now you're playing God?

GRANDPA

I no playing. God is in all of us!

DAN

Great. I haven't got enough problems, now I have to contend with Mel Gibson. *(Pause)* Since when did you become so religious?

GRANDPA

When you reach my age you can ask stupid questions.

DAN

Right! Thanks Dad, I'm really floundering here. I really could use some help.

GRANDPA

You sixty-years-old and want new baby. What you think you gonna do with baby at you age?

Less is More

DAN

I just have a feeling in my gut. Instinct? I don't know. *(Tenderly)* I want to go through a pregnancy with my wife. You know, putting my head on her stomach and listening to the baby move. Didn't you do that Pop?

GRANDPA

That some good reason to have baby at age sixty!

DAN

Michael told me about the most awesome experienced he had as a father. He got the doctor to let him place his hands under his wife while she was giving birth and he caught the baby in his hands as it dropped. (Pause) Can there be a bigger blessing?
(Makes blowing sound to release tension)
Foooof. . . . What was it like, Pop, seeing me, for the first time?

GRANDPA

You want to know truth, you scare me. Looked like wet piece of herring.

DAN

(Laughs)
Go figure. Now I'm the cutest of the bunch.

GRANDPA

(Sarcastically)
You betsha. . . . But what you gonna do with Chris?

DAN

I don't know. I didn't think she would get so upset. It was like I hit a nerve.

GRANDPA

Chris no mention her born parents before?

Baby Boomer Blues

DAN

No. Not sense we told her and Matthew they were adopted, when they were young.

GRANDPA

And Matthew?

DAN

Too busy chasing girls.

GRANDPA

You good with Chris. You can explain everything . . . after you explain everything to me!

DAN

I'm not sure I can explain any more. Isn't it something . . . you just want?

GRANDPA

You betsha. For young man this good and natural, but for older man, not so good and, maybe, not so natural.

DAN

I had a sperm count done and those little suckers are swimming around like they're training for the Olympics.

GRANDPA

Never mind with you jokes. You asked question, I give answer. I remind you what kind of boy you was. Wasn't good for much . . . but . . . good for reading and writing. Not mechanical. You could turn on light switch and turn off radio, but not same time. Not good sports player, but good imagination. Wrote many stories about baseball team you no play on, mountains you never climb . . .

Less is More

DAN

I guess I wanted the freedom to be who I am.

GRANDPA

So, who are you?

DAN

I don't quite know yet.

GRANDPA

Ha! "I don't quite know yet!" You a sixty year old man, and you don't quite know yet? What you waiting for, second coming? With you, I still wait for first! *(Pause)* I know better who you are . . . you . . . younick . . .
(He pronounces it like the word "eunuch")

DAN

Unique!

GRANDPA

You betsha, younick! . . . always you head in clouds . . .

DAN

OK, I think I get the idea. *(Pause)* If "we are such stuff as dreams are made on," then I want to live out my dreams. Having a biological child is my dream and I won't let anyone take it from me.

GRANDPA

God-forbid! God-forbid, Mr. Shakespeare, I should interfere with you dreams.

DAN

I appreciate what you're trying to tell me, only I need to deal with this my own way.

GRANDPA

Go ahead. I wish you good luck, but also good to know the difference between which dreams you can have . . . and which dreams can hurt you . . . and maybe hurt people who love you most.

CHRIS slowly enters through the front door and stops. DAN and CHRIS look at each other in silence.

CHRIS

(From the door)
I forgot to tell Grandpa his "Time Out" was over.
(After pause, she runs to DAN and they hug with great warmth. Lights fade to out.)

CURTAIN

FLIP
By Martin Cohen

Characters

BRENT   An eighteen year old college kid, shy and niave, looking for his first big adventure.

GLORIA   A woman in her thirties, confident and a little brusque.

Time

Present

Setting

A bar in any large city

Flip

Gloria is sitting alone at a small table. There is a full glass of wine on the table that she never touches. Brent is standing at the bar, sees Gloria, picks up his beer, and approaches her table.

BRENT

Hi!
> *(GLORIA looks up. BRENT points to empty chair.)*
> Are you expecting anyone?

GLORIA

Depends.

BRENT

Oh?... Can I join you?

GLORIA

(Looks him over)
> I'm not staying very long.

BRENT

(Sits)
> That's okay, we can share these precious moments together.

GLORIA

Nice!

BRENT

I don't believe in love at first sight, but I'm willing to make an exception in your case.

GLORIA

Oh shit, another crazy. Go away!

Less is More

BRENT

(Points to the bar)
Aah, that guy over there, the guy with the blue shirt, . . . said that it works every time.

GLORIA

That guy over there with the blue shirt is an idiot!

BRENT

(Embarrassed)
Sorry. I'm really sorry. I'm not very good at this . . . I don't . . . I don't have much experience talking to women.

GLORIA

(BRENT stands up to leave. She looks him over.)
Wait. What's your name?

BRENT

Flip, I mean Brent.

GLORIA

Why are you standing there, Flip . . . Brent?
(He sits and after an appropriate pause)
Gloria. I'm Gloria. You looking for a date?

BRENT

A date?

GLORIA

A date for the night.

BRENT

(Getting it)
Aah . . . yes, I guess . . .

Flip

GLORIA

(Ignores BRENTs answer)
What's this "Flip" about?

BRENT

A nickname . . . just a nickname.

GLORIA

Why "Flip"?

BRENT

Well, because I'm good with pinball machine flippers.

GLORIA

Oh you mean you're the Pinball Wizard.

BRENT

No, nothing like that. I'm just really good playing pinball machines. Well I was when I was a kid. Haven't done it for a while . . . years. You know, when I was a kid . . . and the name stuck.

GLORIA

Do you like the name . . FLIP?

BRENT

I don't know, I got used to it. The only ones that call me that are the guys in the neighborhood.

GLORIA

I like it. Do you mind if I call you Flip?

Less is More

BRENT

No, ... I mean if you want.

GLORIA

I like it! It suits you ... in a way. How old are you, Flip?

BRENT

(Offended)
Don't you think I'm old enough ...

GLORIA

Hold on! Don't get your balls in an uproar. I just want to make sure your not jailbait.
(Calls over to the barkeep and points to BRENT)
Harry ...
(A voice from the bar: "The kid's okay.")
How nice. You a college kid?

BRENT

I wish you wouldn't call me "kid."

GLORIA

Sorry ... Flip.

BRENT

Not a problem.
(Looks around bar)
Pretty empty ... for a Friday night. I thought there would be more people here.

GLORIA

It's early. Things get stated around eleven. This is a very specialized bar, pretty exclusive and not very popular with the general public.

Flip

BRENT

Oh?

GLORIA

By the way, how did you hear about Rodney's?

BRENT

Rodney's?

GLORIA

(Points around the bar)
Home sweet home!

BRENT

I don't know. I was looking for a place to come. I was passing by and saw some people standing in front. Looked okay.

GLORIA

That's some recommendation!

BRENT

What do you mean by a specialized bar?

GLORIA

We're just special people who patronize Rodney's. *(Smiles)* Don't give it another thought.

BRENT

I don't mean to be impolite, but I need to know . . . aah . . .

Less is More

GLORIA

How much does a night costs. *(Pause)* Before we do that, I have a confession to make. I have a nickname too . . . "Prettyboy."

BRENT

Pretty . . . BOY?

GLORIA

The only ones that called me that were the guys on the football team. . . . Played Quarterback for Archbishop High School. Never got used to the nickname, but that was a long time ago. *(Pause)* Give me your hand.
(She takes his hand and pulls it under the table)

BRENT

(After an apriopriate pause, he pulls his hand away forcefully and stands)
Oh my God!

GLORIA

Sit down, Flipper! . . . It won't bite.
(Brent slowly sits)
My name was George. I had a wife and two children. Went to church most Sundays and . . . lived a lie . . . my whole life.

BRENT

Why are you telling me all this?

GLORIA

I don't know. Maybe because I have no more secrets, and it feels so freeing. . . . Are you okay?
(BRENT shakes his head, yes)
Not everybody has a understanding ear. Haven't talked about it for a while. You seem . . . well . . .

Flip

BRENT

NO, it's okay, . . . I'm a psych major.
(GLORIA shows pleasant surprise)
Just joking!
(Points to her chest)
You have . . .

GLORIA

Boobs! . . . small but precious. Silicone implants.

BRENT

But the rest is . . .
Unfinished! I'm not ready for surgery down there. Don't know if I ever will be.

BRENT

Can I ask what made you change your . . .

GLORIA

I knew I was a woman since I was nine. I knew . . . inside my head. I had to lie every day. I got sick of lying, trying to keep the terrible secret that I wasn't who I said I was.

BRENT

I think I know what you mean.

GLORIA

George was a lie . . . Gloria has nothing to hide. *(Pause)* I had been thinking about making the change all my life, but couldn't do it . . . until I faced death. Not mine. My wife almost lost her life in an auto accident. Pretty bad. Looking at her in that hospital bed, I imagined my own last breath, my last words: "How could you not do something about it? Why have you wasted you life?" *(Pause)* You need a great sense of humor to get through it all. A star quarterback, eating up the cheers from the stadium crowd. . . .

Less is More

Mister Macho now the Home Coming Queen. Pretty funny if you think about it.

BRENT

I don't know... Were you really him?

GLORIA

Mr. Macho? Yes, I was him... on the outside, and maybe in some part of my soul, but I was her looking out at him, I was always me, Gloria, looking out on Mr. Macho. Confusing, huh? That's how I felt all of my life. If you ask me who I am, I mean what I'm made up of, I will tell you I'm more a woman than a man. My thinking, emotions, all of it, are a woman's.

BRENT

How can you be a woman when you were born a man? Do you have sex with men, because I'm not...

GLORIA

No, I'm not gay. I love women. Have sexual feelings for women, and, at the same time I'm a woman . It's my gender identity. I have to admit, I have a hell of a time explaining to men that I'm not interested. So when I go out socially I only go to places people know me. I live for the companionship of friends.

BRENT

I envy you, in a way, you knowing who you are. I always wondered why I had so much trouble with women... girls, when I was younger. Always got along with guys, and I have to admit I would steal a glance at men when we would shower after phys ed... to see how big they were... just to compare, you know.

GLORIA

Sounds pretty normal to me.

Flip

BRENT

Look who's talking about normal! *(Slight pause)* Sorry, I didn't meant to . . .

GLORIA

Don't be concerned. If I was that sensitive, I'd would never have gotten through it.

BRENT

What I really meant is . . . I don't know what I meant! I don't know who I am, and where I fit in. And for the life of me, I don't understand why . . . why I came here. I just don't get it!

GLORIA

(Long pause. Ignores BRENT's comment.)
 I guess you must be disappointed not getting what you came here for . . .
 (Searches through her purse and takes out a paper and pen and writes a telephone number.)
 Here's Mary's telephone number. Mary is very good with first timers.

BRENT

(Hesitates taking the paper)
 I don't know.

GLORIA

I think you should give it a try. If it doesn't work out, I'd recommend . . . the idiot with the blue shirt. He's really a nice guy!
 (BRENT slowly takes the paper)
 You are Joe College . . . right?

BRENT

Yes.

Less is More

GLORIA

Mary likes college guys. She reads a lot! *(Pause)* And . . . she'll give you a nice discount if you refer a friend.

BRENT

Really?

GLORIA

Just joking!
    (After an appropriate pause, GLORIA reaches both hands across table to BRENT as a gesture of friendship. He hesitates at first, but slowly places his hands in hers.)
    (Lights fade to out)

CURTAIN

TRUE BLUE
by Eliza Roaring Springs

Characters

Janet Corbett   Middle-aged actress, friendly, confident, bright. Physically fit, but always supports her left arm, wears jeans and a pullover.

Dr. Robert Sanders   30 years old. Neurologist, fresh out of his residency. Arrogant, patronizing, always in a hurry.

Setting

Doctor's examination room. His medical degree and diplomas are prominently displayed, in addition to several enlarged photographs of Alaska.

Time

Fall 2005

Less is More

As lights come up, JANET sits alone, waiting for the doctor. She gets up and looks at the diplomas and photos on the walls. DR. SANDERS enters hurriedly, holding a file folder of papers.

DR. SANDERS

(looking at file) Ms. Corbett? uh . . . . Janet? I'm Dr. Sanders.

JANET

Richard? *(referring to diploma on wall)*

DR. SANDERS

No, that was my father.

JANET

Ah, carrying on the family tradition . . .

DR. SANDERS

. . . so to speak. I'm Robert. *(referring to his diploma)*

JANET

When were you there? *(pointing to a photo of the Aurora Borealis)*

DR. SANDERS

Oh, just last year—sort of a "you-finally-graduated" celebration. My fiancee took me— that's her. This one's taken just a little north of Fairbanks.

JANET

You were lucky to get that shot. We camped in Alaska for nearly three months and only saw the Aurora once—it was in the middle of the night and we were half asleep.
Did you photo shop this?

True Blue

DR. SANDERS

Yes, I did. The blues just pop right out, don't they? I'm rather proud of that one.

JANET

But it didn't really look like this.

DR. SANDERS

Well no, I enhanced it. Striking, isn't it?

JANET

Yeah . . . but a little misleading, don't you think? People go there, expecting this—could be disappointing when they see the real thing. It's not really this bright.

DR. SANDERS

But maybe they'll see this because this is what they expect to see. I've made their experience even better.
(*Awkward silence. Janet sits.*)
When were you there?

JANET

Oh, it must have been ten years ago now. It was before I got the diagnosis.

DR. SANDERS

Ah. Well, Janet, I've gotten the results of your tests and I have some very good news for you about that.

JANET

A cure?

DR. SANDERS

No, even better. I've studied the EMG and the nerve conduction assessment, and I am quite certain that you do NOT have fascioscapulohumeral dystrophy.

JANET

It went away?

DR. SANDERS

No. You never had it!

JANET

I don't have muscular dystrophy.

DR. SANDERS

No.

JANET

And you're saying I never have had muscular dystrophy?

DR. SANDERS

Well, muscular dystrophy doesn't just "go away." And we don't have a cure as yet, so . . . no, you never had it.

JANET

Are you kidding me?

DR. SANDERS

Congratulations!

JANET

But those same tests said I did have it ten years ago . . .

True Blue

DR. SANDERS

Yes, but the tests are much more definitive now. With computers we can distinguish the various forms of dystrophy and make more precise and accurate diagnoses.

JANET

Right.
(*Awkward silence.*)

DR. SANDERS

Well, this is very good news, Janet. I will leave a copy of my report for you with the receptionist.
(*He starts to leave.*)

JANET

But it made sense—it fit all my symptoms. Isn't it there in the records? The numbness in my left arm . . . the fireworks in my shoulder . . .

DR. SANDERS

Yes, I have studied Dr. Greens's report thoroughly, and I can see how you might have . . .

JANET

He just looked at me and he knew! He said "Can you whistle?" "No." "Could you do handstands when you were a kid?" "No." "Swing on the monkey bars?" "No." At first I thought he was joking, but then he said he wanted to do some tests—he thought I might have a form of muscular dystrophy.

DR. SANDERS

Well, I really don't understand how Dr. Green could have determined that just by looking at you. Obviously, he was . . .

Less is More

JANET

But the tests proved it! He placed those same little electrodes all over my body just like you did, and he made the muscles contract—it just wasn't all connected to a computer.

JANET (Cont'd)

He moved the little pincers around, flicked a switch, and twitch! Flick, twitch!
Flick, twitch! But then he put them between my shoulder blades and nothing happened. Zip. Nada. So he moved them around a bit and tried again. *Nobody home.* It was creepy AND conclusive. FSH—Fascioscapulohumeral dystrophy. Genetic, degenerative, no cure, no treatment. Bye-bye!

DR. SANDERS

But Janet, we have made tremendous strides in medical research since then, and having access to new technology allows us to present incontrovertible proof! If you would just take a moment to look at these results, you would see . . .
(He tries to show her the papers.)

JANET

(interrupting) Wait a minute, what about my mother? She had shoulder problems just like this! Dr. Green said she must have had FSH too! Her symptoms just didn't get this bad, so it was never diagnosed. It's genetic!

DR. SANDERS

Well, we have a simple blood test now, so we can check your parent's DNA and . . .

JANET

They both died.

True Blue

DR. SANDERS

Oh. Well . . . do you have children? (*looking through folder*) This will be very good news for them.

JANET

No, that didn't seem to be a good idea, given the "circumstances" of my health.

DR. SANDERS

I see.

JANET

Do you, *really?* A lot of life can happen in ten years, Doc.

DR. SANDERS

Well, I realize there may have been some "repercussions" from this inaccurate determination, but overall it's really very . . .

JANET

Some "repercussions", yeah! Nice word. I quit AUDITIONING, for god's sake!
    Do you know what that means? I'm an actress!!! You see, I made the mistake of looking up FSH on the web. I thought more information might be helpful—give me an idea of what I was going to be dealing with. And there were all these horrible pictures of people with "advanced stages"— their faces melted away, emaciated torsos, shoulder blades sticking out like bird's wings. My career was doomed. Oh, I might get a role as a witch in a children's play—later on maybe I could be the hunchback of Notre Dame!

DR. SANDERS

Well . . . now you can start auditioning again!

Less is More

JANET

I'm ten years older, Doc. It makes a big difference in my profession—especially for women.
(Awkward silence.)

DR. SANDERS

Well, I do have another patient waiting . . ..

JANET

My boyfriend left me—oh, that happened the first month. I don't know if it was the prospect of me being ugly, or my looming "dependency" that scared him off. Of course, losing him was actually a benefit of your diagnosis . . . I suppose I should thank you for that.

DR. SANDERS

It was not MY diagnosis!

JANET

Oh that's right, it was Dr. Green's . . . means you're off the hook, doesn't it? Maybe I should see him again.

DR. SANDERS

He retired.

JANET

Of course. And you took his place. Great.

DR. SANDERS

Perhaps it would be better if you talked to the Nurse.
(He starts to leave.)

JANET

Why? Too scary for you—dealing with a real person here?

True Blue

DR. SANDERS

No.
(He sits. Awkward silence.)

JANET

(sees magazine on rack) Well, you could at least take my name off the MDA mailing list! I've been getting that stupid magazine every month for ten years! It just appeared in my mailbox one day—I never even asked for it! All those happy photos of "Jerry and the kids". You see, I was an official member of the "club"—a *person with muscular dystrophy.* Do you have any idea what that's really like? It was my identity!

DR. SANDERS

I realize, of course, that it will take time for you to adjust to this new information, but I really think that you . . .

JANET

. . ..should be happy? Of course I'm happy. I'm ecstatic! I just found out that I have spent the last decade of my life based on bullshit—why wouldn't I be happy? Most people probably don't know WHY they've been doing what they've been doing!

Why did you become a doctor, Robert? pleasing Daddy?
(He starts to leave again.)
AND I started eating meat! I HATE MEAT! I was a vegetarian for twenty-five years, but no, muscle is protein, I thought, I have to build up my muscles! Meat is disgusting.

And I have spent a lot of money on meat!

DR. SANDERS

Well, you don't have to eat it anymore!!!

JANET

But why should I believe YOU any more than I should have believed HIM? This is crazy!!!

Less is More

DR. SANDERS

The only thing crazy here is you! If you would just look at these findings, you'll see . . .

(*He opens his folder to show her the report, Janet flips it out of his hand and papers go flying everywhere.*)

JANET

I DON'T WANT TO SEE YOUR NUMBERS!!!

DR. SANDERS

No. It appears you don't.
(*He starts picking up the papers.*)

JANET

I just want you to LISTEN to me!!!
(*He stops.*)

DR. SANDERS

Very well.
(*Prolonged silence.*)
Perhaps you should get a second opinion. Of course, if you'd gotten one ten years ago . . .

JANET

I KNOW! I know. That was so stupid of me. Everybody gets a second opinion. So why didn't I? Because I don't DO western medicine! That isn't me! I'd gone to a chiropractor, an acupuncturist and a massage therapist for more than a year before coming to see Dr. Green. But none of those things were making a difference, and my friend at work said he was worried it could be something serious—like cancer, and shouldn't I go to a real MD, just to be sure. So I did. And I liked Dr. Green and his funny old machines. And his answers all made sense, awful as they were. It all added up—the not whistling . . . the fireworks . . . my mom. It was kind of a relief—it was an *answer*.

And I guess a bad answer felt better than no answer at all.

True Blue

DR. SANDERS

I can recommend one of my colleagues, if you'd like to discuss it with someone else.

JANET

No. I didn't want any more doctors or tests or explanations back then, and I still don't.
    I really hate these places. I can live with my weird shoulder. Mom did.

DR. SANDERS

Of course.
    (*starting to leave*)

JANET

But I'm afraid I may have played up the noble martyr role a bit—it's kind of embarrassing.

DR. SANDERS

But you really believed you had FSH!

JANET

Yeah, and Dr. Green did too. Except I was making it real. I swear my face has been sagging . . .

DR. SANDERS

Probably just age.

JANET

Oh, thanks a lot!
    (*He looks at his watch and rises.*)
    No, really . . . thanks.

Less is More

DR. SANDERS

Janet, I . . ..I am sorry.
(She nods, and he opens the door to leave.)

JANET

(stopping him) Hey, Doc, do you still have the original of that photo?
(He looks back at the Aurora photograph.)

DR. SANDERS

Yes, I do. And actually I've been thinking about trying a color spectrum reversal on it— it'd really heighten the intensity, don't you think?
(She rolls her eyes in disgust.)
It's a JOKE! I think a print of the real thing might look better.
(They laugh, and he opens the door for her.)
Welcome to the rest of your life, Ms. Corbett.

JANET

Oy vey . . .
(He follows her out.)

END OF PLAY.

SISTERS
by Eliza Roaring Springs

Characters

CATHY 16, youngest of three girls, cute, smart, dramatic, "successful" but rebellious by nature

GEORGIE 21, the middle child, a tomboy, glasses, very fit, usually shy and serious, but excited and nervous about her upcoming wedding

Setting

Backyard patio of the Sherman family in southern California.

Time

The night before Georgie's wedding.

Less is More

As lights come up, CATHY is sitting in a chaise lounge on the patio with an afghan wrapped around her, writing in her journal.

GEORGIE

(entering, waving her hands in the air, drying her nails)
It's cold out here! It better be nice tomorrow. What are you writing?
(looking over CATHY's shoulder; CATHY closes her book)

CATHY

Just stuff.

GEORGIE

(sitting on end of the chaise lounge)
You're smart to be out here—it's nuts inside—flowers and ribbons everywhere. Maybe it was a mistake having mom's Ladies Guild make the table decorations.

CATHY

mm hm.

GEORGIE

I don't know what to wear to this thing—I hate clothes! Mom says I should look "special"—whatever that means. But didn't we say tonight was casual? It was even on the invitation. But of course Tom's mother will probably wear a "casual" linen suit—pale pink. I don't think she even owns a pair of pants.
(CATHY smiles.)
Do you think I should wear my hair up tomorrow? The veil looks better without all this frizz sticking out every which way, but then the hat won't fit. I guess I should have gotten a hair appointment after all. Will you fix it?

CATHY

George—I can't do it.

Sisters

GEORGIE

You can't fix my hair? *(CATHY rolls her eyes)* Get dressed up? You don't have to! It's casual—you can go as you are. Well, you could put on real shoes. You'll look cuter than everybody else anyway no matter what you wear. It's disgusting. I just wish we'd held out for having this dinner at the pizza parlor.

CATHY

I can't go.

GEORGIE

... to the dress rehearsal?

CATHY

Yeah.

GEORGIE

But if you don't go tonight you won't know what to do tomorrow. I know you're quick,
    but...

CATHY

Well, that's just it, I don't think I can go to that either.

GEORGIE

... to the WEDDING??? But you're my maid of honor!

CATHY

I know, but I've thought about that, and Judy can do it! She'd love it. Her dress is the same, except for the sash, and she's hot for Ron anyway...

GEORGIE

... the Best Man?? But I thought YOU liked him!

CATHY

No, HE likes ME. And I like that he takes me rock climbing.

GEORGIE

But Cath, this is my WEDDING! You HAVE to be there!
(CATHY shrugs in response.)
You're joking, right? Please tell me you're joking.

CATHY

I'm sorry, George. I just can't do it.

GEORGIE

BUT WHY??? I know you don't like Tom very much, but he's really fun when . . .

CATHY

(shaking her head) It's not Tom. He's fine—he's not for you—but he's OK. It's just everything about it. Why are you marrying him???

GEORGIE

Because I love him!

CATHY

(rolling her eyes) Oh, please . . . you know that won't last. Look at Mom and Dad—they were probably "in love" too, and look how they turned out!

GEORGIE

We're nothing like Mom and Dad!!!

CATHY

OK, you're different . . . and you're in love . . . and you want to get away from here! I get that! So move out! Get your own place—find your *self*, Georgie . . . get to know Tom in the "Biblical sense". You're legal, you can do that! no matter what Dad says. And what happened to us living together someday? I only have one more year of high school, and then we can go to San Francisco like we always said—I can write, you can be an artist, or P.E. teacher or something . . . anything you want!

GEORGIE

Oh Cath, that was just a childhood fantasy, like in some novel.

CATHY

No, what you're doing now is a fantasy! Marrying the nice Christian guy who's going to be an engineer and make a "good living" someday. You'll get a boring house somewhere in the suburbs and have babies. Oh, and you can do lots of church work with his mother. Whoopie!

GEORGIE

I like doing church work!

CATHY

I know . . . but what about getting your Master's?

GEORGIE

I can still go back to school someday!

CATHY

But you won't. Bet you a hundred bucks! You'll get pregnant, and he won't let you.

GEORGIE

He's not like that! You don't even know Tom.

CATHY

And you DO? What? You've been "seeing" each other for a year now? Almost always at church functions. Real opportunity for deep talks there!

And it's not like you have a lot to compare him with—you only had two dates in high school. You're still a virgin, Georgie! What if he's a lousy lover, and you're stuck with him? FOREVER!!!!

GEORGIE

He won't be!!

CATHY

But how do you know???
(Awkward silence.)

GEORGIE

I don't. But we'll figure it out.

CATHY

You can't even COOK! You've always been outside with Dad—fixing the car, painting the house, putting in this patio! You think Tom's going to cook? I doubt it—not the way his mother's been doting on him all his life. You'll starve!

GEORGIE

(laughing) We'll order takeout! or live on Top Ramen, or we can hire YOU to be our cook! Come on, Cath. It'll be OK . . . really. Let's go get ready. I know, we'll wear pajamas!

CATHY

Georgie, I'm serious! This is a bad idea. WHY are you doing this??? Did your biological clock just go off or something? "time to get married"! Are you afraid no one else will ever ask you—like this is your only shot at it?

GEORGIE

And what could you possibly know about that? Little "Miss Friendship of Orange County"—straight A student—Homecoming princess!!! Maybe you just don't want ME to be the center of attention for once! Well, you're not going to ruin this for me.

CATHY

I don't want to, George. That's why I'm not coming.

GEORGIE

I can't believe you're doing this right now—the night before the wedding! We've been planning this for months.

CATHY

Well, I thought I could do it for you. I was really trying to be a trouper . . .

GEORGIE

But you were OK at the bridal shower—you even organized the games!

CATHY

Just cause I knew they'd be really stupid if I didn't.

GEORGIE

Well, everybody else is really happy for me, and they think we're a perfect couple!

CATHY

That's because they have the same "white picket fence" fantasy! And none of them really know you—not like I do. Mom thinks you've finally found your true "womanly self" cause you polish your nails and have a boyfriend—excuse me, *fiancee*. Makes me puke. And God only knows what Dad thinks, but I bet he's jealous. He's gonna miss your help around here, and I'm sure not stepping in!

GEORGIE

Cath, why are you being like this?

Less is More

CATHY

Because I love you, you stupid idiot! You're my hero—don't you know that?? You're the one who climbed the highest tree . . . who jumped off the roof when we weren't supposed to! You taught me how to ride a bicycle . . . and you gave me that toy microscope when I thought I wanted to be a doctor. And you're not afraid of anything—mice, jellyfish, even Dad when he's drinking. You're the only one who stands up to him.

He HATES me, and I hate him.

GEORGIE

We're not moving that far away, Cath—just across town. And if it gets too bad here with Dad you can come live with us. Really. I already talked to Tom about it.
(CATHY shakes her head no.)
It'll be OK, Cath, you'll see. When you get older, you'll understand.

CATHY

Don't do that, George, don't pull that "wiser older sister" crap on me. God, you sound like Mom. Big 21-year-old college graduate with a shiny diamond on her finger—showing what a good "catch" she's made. I hope I never understand that.
(Silence.)
What's happened to you? Ever since you got back from Mexico last summer you've been different. I know you really got into the Jesus thing with those missionaries down there, but it's more than that . . .

GEORGIE

It's just they . . ..the Emerys helped me sort some things out . . .

CATHY

like what?

GEORGIE

like . . . like not giving in to stuff.

Sisters

CATHY

like . . .

GEORGIE

. . . like impure thoughts and deeds. Things that aren't good for me.

CATHY

. . . like . . . smoking that joint?

GEORGIE

yeah, that. And other things . . .
(prolonged silence)

CATHY

. . . like making out with Donna!!! THAT'S IT, ISN'T IT?

GEORGIE

What????

CATHY

You really LIKED it! I knew it!!!!

GEORGIE

WHAT? So you think I'm a lesbian??? is that what this is all about? Cause I got silly once and kissed your girlfriend? well, she kissed me first! And we were just fooling around . . .

CATHY

Donna didn't think so.

Less is More

GEORGIE

So, were you going to announce it at the wedding? When the preacher says "if anyone has just cause why this man and woman should not be joined together in holy matrimony, let him speak now . . ."

CATHY

I wouldn't say you were a lesbian! I don't even know that, for sure. But I would say "This is a BIG mistake!!!" and then Dad would pull out his gun and shoot me and spray blood all over your white dress!

GEORGIE

Yeah! and it'd be in all the papers and you'd upstage me again!
(They laugh and hug.)
Mom and Dad will freak out if you don't come.

CATHY

Nah, they'll be relieved. Now they won't have to worry about me doing something that might embarrass them.

GEORGIE

Well, that's true.
(CATHY punches her.)

CATHY

I'm sorry you had to have that dress made for me.

GEORGIE

You can still have it—keep it for the prom or something—fits you perfect.

CATHY

Nah. Somehow I don't think there's another prom in my future. So, you're really going to go through with this, huh?

Sisters

GEORGIE

Yeah, might as well. Everybody's coming. Even Aunt Cora . . ..

GEORGIE & CATHY (together)

. . . "all the way from St. Louis!"

GEORGIE

And what else would I do with all those ugly table decorations? I know you don't get it, Cath, but I have to do this.

CATHY

Yeah, and I have to do this.

GEORGIE

You know, you don't look so good. *(feeling Cathy's forehead)* And I think you have a fever.

CATHY

Yeah, I'm feeling kind of pukey all of a sudden.

GEORGIE

There's that flu bug going around . . . be terrible if you gave it to everybody. *(She tucks the afghan around her.)* I'll tell Mom.
(GEORGIE starts to leave.)

CATHY

Hey George—have fun.

END OF PLAY

www.ingramcontent.com/pod-product-compliance
Lightning Source LLC
Chambersburg PA
CBHW070303100426
42743CB00011B/2325